Nighttime Animals

Penguin
Random
House

LONDON, NEW YORK, MUNICH,
MELBOURNE, and DELHI

Series Editor Deborah Lock
US Senior Editor Shannon Beatty
Art Director Martin Wilson
Designer Yamini Panwar
Picture Researcher Surya Sarangi
Producer, Pre-production Francesca Wardell
Jacket Designer Martin Wilson

Reading Consultant
Linda Gambrell, Ph.D.

First American Edition, 2015
Published in the United States by DK Publishing
345 Hudson Street, New York, New York 10014

15 16 17 18 19 10 9 8 7 6 5 4 3 2 1
001—270550—February/15

A catalog record for this book is available
from the Library of Congress.

ISBN: 978-1-4654-2852-3 (Paperback)
ISBN: 978-1-4654-2853-0 (Hardcover)

DK books are available at special discounts when purchased in bulk for sales promotions,
premiums, fund-raising, or educational use. For details, contact:
DK Publishing Special Markets
345 Hudson Street, New York, New York 10014
SpecialSales@dk.com

Printed and bound in China by South China Printing Company

The publisher would like to thank the following for their kind permission to reproduce their photographs:
(Key: a=above, b=below/bottom, c=center, l=left, r=right, t=top)

1 naturepl.com: Ingo Arndt (c). **6 Corbis:** Tom Brakefield (c). **6–7 Alamy Images:** John Pitcher/Design Pics Inc.
8 Alamy Images: Rolf Nussbaumer Photography. **9 naturepl.com:** Markus Varesvuo. **10 Alamy Images:** Radius Images (c).
10–11 Science Photo Library: Dr. John Brackenbury. **12 Corbis:** Ocean (ca). **12–13 Alamy Images:** Phillip Ross (b).
14–15 Alamy Images: Joe McDonald/Steve Bloom Images. **16 naturepl.com:** Ian Lockwood (c). **17 Corbis:** Lin Yiguang/
Xinhua Press. **18–19 Corbis:** Rolf Nussbaumer/imagebroker. **20 Alamy Images:** Elizabeth Czitronyi (cb). **20–21 Science
Photo Library:** B. G. Thomson. **22 Corbis:** Kim Taylor/Nature Picture Library. **23 naturepl.com:** Barry Mansell (c).
24–25 Corbis: Mark Jones/Minden Pictures. **26–27 Corbis:** Gianluca Perris/National Geographic Society.
27 Getty Images: Beverly Joubert/National Geographic (c).**28 Getty Images:** Picture by Tambako the Jaguar/
Flickr Open (cb). **28–29 Photoshot:** Joe McDonald/Woodfall (ca). **29 Corbis:** Ocean (cl). **naturepl.com:** Paul Harcourt
Davies (cr). **30 Alamy Images:** Elizabeth Czitronyi (tl), Life on white (cla); **Corbis:** Hal Beral (clb), Ocean (cl);
naturepl.com: Markus Varesvuo (bl). Inside back cover: **naturepl.com:** Markus Varesvuo (br).

Jacket images: *Front:* **Getty Images:** David Haring / DUPC / Oxford Scientific

All other images © Dorling Kindersley
For further information see: www.dkimages.com

Discover more at
www.dk.com

Contents

The sun sets.
The nighttime animals
wake up.
It's time to eat.

Coyotes

Coyotes run and hunt.
They call to each other.

Howl!

Owls

talon

wing

Swoosh!

Owls look and listen.
Then they swoop in
to catch an animal.

Moths

luna moths

Moths fly around
in the moonlight.

red underwing
moth

Scorpions

stinger

claw

Scorpions lift
their stingers.
They are ready
to attack.

Boa constrictors

Slither!

A boa constrictor
slithers along
a branch.
It searches for food.

scaly skin

Lorises

Lorises see in the dark with wide-open eyes.

eye

fingers

Raccoons

Raccoons scamper
around the logs.
They will eat any food
they can find.

fur

Possums

Possums scurry around with their joeys.

joey

Bats

Squeak!

Bats fly around
at night.
They squeak
through their noses.

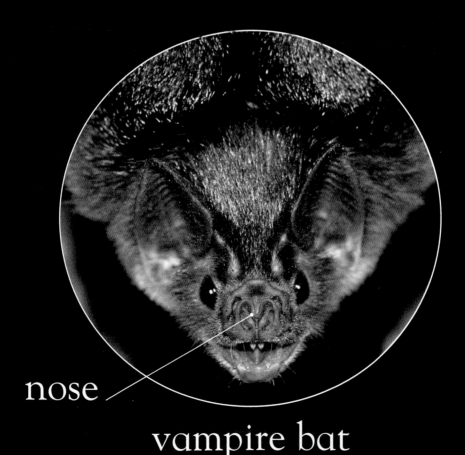

nose

vampire bat

Aardvarks

Aardvarks smell
the ants and termites
they like to eat.

Sniff! Sniff!

snout

Leopards

A leopard hunts alone.
Its glowing eyes
can see very well.

ear

eye

The sun rises.
The nighttime
animals sleep.
It's been a busy night.

Glossary

Joey
young possum, kangaroo, or wallaby

Snout
long nose and mouth of an animal

Stinger
stinging part of an insect

Talon
sharp claw of a bird

Wing
flying arm of a bird covered with large feathers

Index

Have you read these other great books from DK?

LEARNING TO READ

Croak! M... ...Chatter! Meet the... Please... ...d have fun!
closer ... ...colorful
the f... ...oughout
toads o... ...ear.

Dead...
Dino...
Niki Foreman

Roar! ... ...ts on!
the ... ...e busy
Who ... ...s build
is the ... ...chool.